Dear Reader . . .

Guess who Mama just heard from?

Right.

Her son, the camper.

And every precious ink-smudged misspelled word has been recorded for posterity. And for Aunt Harriet, Grandma, Cousin Ben and Mrs. Whatshername next door. And you.

Because with this book, even if you have never sprung an off-spring on an unsuspecting summer camp, you'll still be on the receiving end of some of the funniest and wildest special deliveries ever brought back alive from Uncle Sammy's post office.

—The Editors

LETTERS
FROM
CAMP

By BILL ADLER

Author of
KIDS' LETTERS TO PRESIDENT KENNEDY

With cartoons by
SYD HOFF

MB

A MACFADDEN BOOK

A MACFADDEN BOOK . . . 1962

Copyright, ©, 1961 by Bill Adler and Syd Hoff
Library of Congress Catalogue Card Number 61-9022
All rights reserved
Published by arrangement with Chilton Company, Publishers

MACFADDEN BOOKS are published by
MACFADDEN-BARTELL CORPORATION
205 East 42nd Street, New York 17, New York

PRINTED IN CANADA

DEDICATION

To my bunkmates at Camp Equinunk and Camp Chipinaw and especially to Mel Barasch who still hasn't returned the left sneaker he borrowed 15 summers ago. Come on, Mel!

A Note of Explanation

We have divided the letters and postcards in this book into subjects.

For example, all those letters dealing with the counselor are filed under the chapter so indicated. We believe that this will make it easier for most parents to find their own children.

You will notice that most of the letters in this book are very short. There is a reason for that. It seems to be an unwritten law among our children that, if you can't say it in less than 25 words, don't say it at all.

Most of us parents are so grateful for any sort of correspondence from our children that we don't even bother to count.

P.S. You will find an occasional note from the counselor himself in this book. We felt that this was only right. Equal time is an American tradition.

This book is dedicated to the hundreds of thousands of Mothers and Fathers who save their hard-earned money all winter to send their children to camp each summer so that their youngsters can enjoy those precious weeks in the sun.

And their reward? All any parent ever asks in return is an occasional letter or postcard.

"Please write to us, Billy." Do Billy and Bobby and Susan write? Sometimes.

And when they do write, their letters from camp become priceless documents recording the growth, the tears, the joys, and the frustrations of our children.

Some of our greatest writers showed the first signs of their talent in letters from camp.

Perhaps nestled away today at some camp in the Adirondack Mountains is tomorrow's Paddy Chayefsky, Fannie Hurst, or James Michener.

So, in the interest of the future literary heritage of America, we present, unedited and in their original form, many of the most wonderful letters from camp.

Contents

Letters from Camp

1. The Counselor

It is natural for a child to hate his counselor on Monday, love him on Tuesday, and be uncertain about him on Wednesday.

Counselors represent, at various times, Mother, Father, authority, and companionship. That's a tall order for any individual!

So think kindly of the counselor. Imagine—they take care not only of your child but six more like him. Want the job?

Dear Mom and Dad,

Next summer I want to be a counselor so someone will row me around the lake. I am tired.

Love and xxxxx,

STEWART

Dear Folks,

Yesterday our counselor told us all about where babies come from. You lied to me.

Love and xxxxx,

MARGARET

Dear Mom and Dad,

We all get up at 6:30 AM here at camp except our counselor who has trouble hearing the bugle. He should see a doctor. Don't you think so?

Love,

SIS

CAMPER'S PROGRESS REPORT

From: Robert's counselor

To: Mr. and Mrs. Johnson

Baseball   B
Football   B+
Basketball   C
Gets along with bunkmates   B
Eating   B
Swimming   B
Toilet habits   F

17

Dear Folks,

I learned how to make a bed. The counselor taught me how to make his. Aren't you proud of me?

Love,

JEFFREY

Dear Folks,

I like my counselor. Last night for dinner he let me have a peanut butter and cucumber sandwich instead of a lamb chop.

Love and xxxxx,

DANNY

Dear Folks,

Yesterday we put a frog in my counselor's bed. He got mad. I don't like my counselor. He's not a good sport.

Love,

JOHN

Dear Mom and Dad,

Every day at meal time we say our prayers that we can get at the steak before the counselor does.

Love,

BILLY

Dear Dad,

My counselor's name is fathead.

Love,

WYN

Dear Dad,

I don't like my counselor. He is always hitting us.
Last night we threw his sneakers in the lake and he
hit us again.

GEORGE

Dear Mom,

The counselor said if you don't slide into first base right, you could break your leg. Now I know what he means.

Love,

MICHAEL

Dear Mom,
  I drew a picture of my counselor for you.
        (*Picture of Skull and Crossbones*)
                                    MITCHELL

Dear Folks,
  Don't send me any more candy. My counselor made me write this letter.

                        Love,

                                    VIVIAN

Dear Folks,
  Last night there was a fire in the camp. Nobody was hurt except the counselor that was smoking in bed.
                        Your daughter,

                                    DIANA

Dear Dad,
  Remember when my counselor came to visit us in the city before camp started and he said he liked little boys like me. Well, he doesn't.

                                    JOHN

Dear Mom,
  We have a terrific counselor. He lets us have ice cream and frankfurters for breakfast. He is nicer than the counselor last year that made us eat cereal. Please send him a big tip.

                        Love,

                                    JERRY

To His Big Sister

Dear Sis,

I showed your picture to my counselor. He thinks you're pretty. If you send me $1.00 I won't tell him that you wear braces on your teeth.

PETE

Same Boy, One Day Later

Dear Sis,

Never mind the dollar. My counselor just saw a picture of Bobby Amron's sister.

PETE

Dear Folks,

I was the best boy in the bunk this week so I got to bring the counselor his breakfast in bed.

Your son,

JORDAN

Dear Mom and Dad,

Our counselor is very nice to us. Please send him a big tip so he won't sock us anymore.

Love,

FRANK

Dear Folks,

This camp would be fun if they didn't have any counselors.

Love,

MIKE

Dear Mom and Dad,

I have written a poem about our counselor.

Spaghetti on meat balls,
Ice cream on cake,
Our counselor should drown in the lake.

Love,

ROGER

Dear Mom and Dad,

Our counselor tells us a story every night before we go to bed. Last night he told us about how he almost captured Hitler by himself.

KENNETH

2. Love

Kids discover all sorts of things at camp. One of them is love. Some kids fall in love with rabbits, others with girls or boys. Some even fall in love with butterflies.

If your child should write to say that he has fallen in love with a yellow-winged butterfly, don't worry—it won't last. After all, did you ever hear of anyone going to a butterfly's wedding?

Same Girl Three Weeks in a Row

1ST WEEK

Dear Mother,

I met a wonderful boy at the dance and someday I'm going to marry him.

2ND WEEK

Dear Mother,

I met a new boy at the dance who I am going to marry. I really mean it.

3RD WEEK

Dear Mother,

I met a boy at the dance this Saturday who is wonderful. I'm going to marry him for sure.

Dear Mom,

I am sending you a butterfly that I caught for your birthday.

Love,

JANE

From a Boy at Camp to His Girlfriend at Another Camp

Dear Betty,

   I am having fun. Are you? Yesterday I hit a home run. None of the girls at this camp are as pretty as you are. Are any of the boys at your camp as good-looking as me? Please answer soon.

Your boyfriend,
ALAN EDWARDS

Her Answer

Dear Alan,

   No, none of the boys are as good-looking as you are. There are none at this camp. See you soon.

Your girlfriend,
BETTY

Dear Folks,

   I have fallen in love with a girl. She is the Camp Mother. Do you think she is too old for me?

Love,
JIM

Dear Mom and Dad,

   I met a nice girl. Her name is Nancy. She lives on River Street. When I come home I want to marry her. Please send me 60 cents for an engagement ring.

Love,
MIKE

Dear Mom and Dad,

> Roses are Red
> Violets are Blue
> Do you miss me
> Like I miss you?

LUCILLE

Three Letters by a Young Lady to Her "Boyfriend" at Home

1ST LETTER

Dear Robert,

None of the boys here are as good looking as you.

2ND LETTER

Dear Robert,

There is one boy here who is almost as good looking as you.

3RD LETTER

Dear Robert,

I can't see you anymore.

Dear Grandma,

Before we go to sleep, we say our prayers, I pray for you every night. Do you think you could send me a new baseball glove?

Love,
YOUR GRANDDAUGHTER LOUISE

A Little Girl to Her Brother

Dear Brother,

I am enclosing a picture of my bunkmate, Gloria. Isn't she pretty? She is my best friend up here. Would you like to meet her? She knows how to play softball. Have you met any boys for me? I hope so. I don't want to be an old maid like Cousin Gertrude.

Love,

YOUR SISTER

Dear Mom,

I met a very pretty girl along the nature path while we were hunting snakes. Where did you meet Dad?

Love,

ANDREW

Dear John,

I don't love you anymore. I met someone else here at camp. I am sending the skate key you gave me back. I am sorry. You will find another girl who skates.

Your friend,

ELLEN

To His Dog

Dear Skippy,

I miss you very much. Do you miss me? I will be home soon, and then I will take you out. Please wait.

Love,

ALLEN

To Her Girlfriend at Another Camp

Dear Sandra,

None of the boys at this camp are cute. Are they cute at your camp? Maybe next summer I will go to your camp if the boys are cute. Are they? I must know.

Love,

LAURA

ANSWER

Dear Laura,

Forget it. I was planning to go to your camp next summer.

SANDRA

Dear Mom and Dad,

I met a terrific girl at the camp dance. She is a first baseman like me.

Love,

ARTHUR

Dear Folks,

Our counselor has told us about the birds and the bees. I don't believe in the stork anymore.

ELLEN

For some reason, children seem to age at camp. You send them away as kids and they return as men or women of the world.

They become smarter, more mature, more developed. You'll be proud when they return. But don't let on. They charge extra for that!

Dear Mom and Dad,

I don't like camp any more. Next summer I want to go to the moon instead.

Love,

ARNOLD

Dear Mrs. Amron,

I know that you will be happy to hear that your son, Howard, does not wet his bed any more. We find that depriving him of water for three or four days is very helpful. I hope you will be happy with the progress we are making.

Sincerely,

HOWARD'S COUNSELOR

Dear Mom and Dad,

I ran out of comic books. Please send three Dick Tracy, four L'il Abner and two Peanuts comic books. Don't send any more Mickey Mouse comics. I don't like them any more. They are very silly.

Love,

JOAN

Dear Folks,

Last night we had a spelling bee and I won. I am the best speller in the camp. Aren't you proud of me? We will have another spelling bee next Wededay.

Love,

YOUR SUN PETER

Dear Folks,

My friend Mitch and I have a good deal. When we go on an overnight hike I carry his pack up the hill and he carries mine when we go down.

Your son,

FRED

Dear Folks,

I am sending you twenty postcards today so I won't have to write for the rest of the summer.

Love,

MONTE

Dear Dad,

If this camp cost more than $20 you were gyped.

Love,

MICHAEL

Dear Mom and Dad,

I found a quick way to make my bed. I sleep on the covers.

Love,

MARILYN

Dear Mom,

All the girls in my bunk wear lipstick. Can't I? Please send me written permission airmail special delivery. I have to show it to my counselor right away because I started last Saturday.

Love,

JEAN

Dear Mom,

Next week it is my turn to clean the bunk. Please send me your vaccuum cleaner.

Love,

MELVIN

Dear Folks,

Look what they wrote about me in the camp newspaper. I am also the editor of the camp newspaper.

Love and xxx,

EVELYN

Dear Mom and Dad,

I learned to dress myself. Yesterday it was very hot and I put on my sweater and lumber jacket and long pants without any help.

JOSHUA

Dear Mom and Dad,

Next summer I don't want to go to camp. I want to go to Europe and climb Mount Everest.

Love,

DEAN

From the moment most youngsters leave for camp, their parents worry about their health. Suppose they get hurt or sick—who will take care of them?

Relax—camps are masters at handling all sorts, shapes, and types of childhood maladies, including poison ivy, mumps, measles, and homesickness.

If your child should have to have his appendix out while at camp, don't worry. The next day he will be back on the baseball diamond—who knows?—maybe even during the operation.

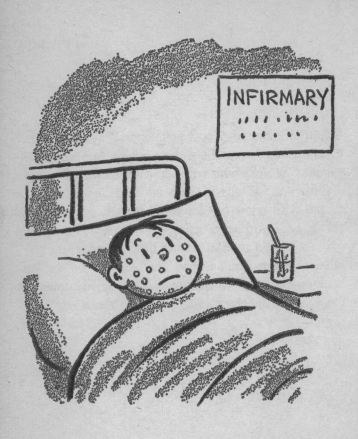

Dear Folks,

Please don't touch this postcard because I have the measles and you might get them, too. Did you ever have the measles?

Love,

JOHN

Dear Dad,

You will be proud of me. Yesterday when we played baseball, I caught the ball with my bare right hand.

Love,

LEFTY

Dear Mom,

Here is a picture they took of all the boys in the bunk. I am the one with his arm in the sling.

JEFF

Dear Mom and Dad,

Every time we brush our teeth right we get a point. I owe six points.

Love,

BARBARA

Dear Mom and Dad,

Guess what? The doctor says I have athlete's feet. I guess I really am a good baseball player.

Love,

DAN

41

Dear Mom,

Jackie Peters, my bunkmate, is writing this letter for me because I wrote for him when he broke his hand.

ALVIN

Dear Folks,

Dr. Braunstein was wrong. You can get mumps twice.

Love,

LARRY

Three Letters from the Same Boy

1ST LETTER

Dear Mom,

I lost a few pounds.

2ND LETTER

Dear Mom,

I lost a few more pounds.

3RD LETTER

Dear Mom,

Guess what I weigh now?

ARNOLD

Dear Mom and Dad,

Please don't worry. I'm learning to eat and write with my other hand.

FRANK

Dear Mom and Dad,

Yesterday I had an examination and I am in 100% good health. My bunkmate, Ted, examined me. He is going to be a doctor.

Love,

EDDIE

Dear Folks,

Here is a picture of me with my best friend, Peter. He looks funny because he has the measles.

Your son,

DONALD

Dear Folks,

Here is a picture of me that one of the boys took. I am not smiling in the picture because I didn't want you to worry about the two front teeth that are missing.

DAVID

Dear Mom and Dad,

I cannot lie to you. I am not fine. I have 103 degree temperature and I broke my leg. But don't worry. At least I didn't get Chicken Pox like the other kids in my bunk.

Your son,

NORMAN

Dear Mom and Dad,
   I don't bite my nails any more because I broke my hand.

                              Love,

                                        GLORIA

What parent hasn't said to his children as they depart for camp: "Eat well, Betty, it's costing us a lot of money!"

Naturally some kids eat better than others. If your child happens to be one of the bad eaters, don't fret—nature has a way of compensating. He probably drinks a lot of water.

Dear Mom and Dad,

I like the desserts here. Today for lunch I had apple pie, jello, chocolate pudding, and ice cream. What did you eat today?

Love,

BILLY

Dear Mom and Dad,

I miss you very much. Please send your picture with a box of candy.

Love,

JOAN

Dear Mom and Dad,

The food is very bad here. I am enclosing a lamb chop to show you what I mean.

Love,

JIMMY

Dear Folks,

I am saving you a lot of money because I am not eating lunch.

Love,

ELAINE

Dear Uncle Louie,

Could you send me a watermelon or a gallon of ice cream? Whichever is easier.

Love,

CHARLOTTE

Dear Folks,

I miss Mommy's cooking. They don't serve cold potatoes here.

Love,

BOBBY

Dear Folks,

You will be happy to know I have not eaten in three days so I lost nine pounds. Aren't you glad?

Your daughter,

MELISSA

Dear Folks,

Today for supper we had vegetable soup, steak, french fried potatoes, carrots, ice cream and cake. Please send me a package of food. I am starved.

Love,

RONALD

Dear Folks,

Every day when I sit down to eat I say my prayers first like you told me to. Only when I finish my prayers and look up all the meat is gone already.

Love,

CHARLES

Dear Mom,

Last week you sent me a bag that had 1,826 indian nuts. This week the bag had 1,820 indian nuts. Please send the six missing nuts right away.

JOEL

Dear Folks,

    Remember how I used to hate Spinach? Well, they serve Spinach here and I still hate it.

Love,

BEATRICE

Dear Mom,

When Daddy went to camp did you send him candy, too?

Love,

HENRY

Dear Mom,

Please send me a glass of chocolate milk. They only have plain milk here.

Love,

PATRICIA

Dear Mother,

Please have a big dinner ready for me when I get home. I haven't eaten all summer.

Love and xxx,

FRANK

Dear Mom and Dad,

It has been three days since you sent me a package. You are starving me.

YOUR EX-SON

6. Writing Home

We have been told that even William Shakespeare didn't like to write letters. So what can you expect from a lesser mortal?

Besides, we put great demands on our youngsters when we send them to camp. We usually insist that, in addition to writing to us daily, they write to:

> Grandma
> Grandpa
> Aunt Sadie
> Uncle John
> Cousin Paul
> Cousin Jack
> Etc.
> Etc.

It's getting so bad that one kid asked his father's secretary to come up with him. At any rate, here is how they have handled the situation.

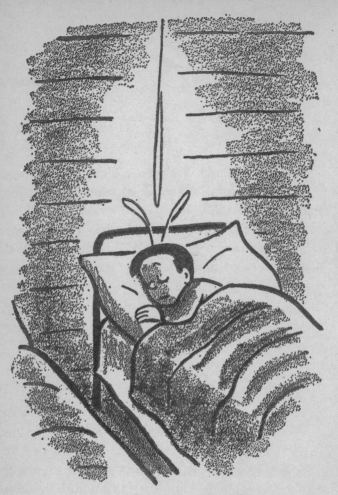

Written on the First Day of Camp

Dear Mom,

They put me in the same bunk as before because the roof leaks over my head like last year.

HOWARD

Dear Folks,

The baseball glove you send me is no good. Yesterday I made three errors in the game. Please send me a new glove quick.

JONATHAN

Dear Aunt Martha,

Thank you for the cake you baked and sent me. Next time could you send me a cake from the store?

Love,

ANITA

Dear Folks,

One of the boys broke his leg. They had a big fire in the recreation hall. My counselor had his appendix out. The boy in the bed next to me almost drowned. The water pipe broke in the kitchen and they had a flood. A tree fell down when the lightening hit it and they found a big rat in one of the bunks. Nothing else is new.

Love,

PETER

Dear Uncle Herb,

Mommy told me you are coming up to see me next week. Here is a list of the comic books I don't have.

Dick Tracy Gets the Spy
Bugs Bunny in the Forest
Captain Midnight Rides Again
Superman Versus the Batman
Tarzan and the Apes
Robin Hood's Big Adventure

I just need one of each.

Your nephew,

SIDNEY

Dear Dad,

Don't give my counselor a tip until he gives me back the live lobster I caught.

LESTER

Dear Folks,

It's too expensive to write you every day so I am going to save money and call you instead.

Love,

JANET

Dear Dad,

I get tired writing letters all the time. Please send your secretary up.

Love,

ANITA

Dear Mother,
 I am saving all my dirty laundry for you.
                    Love,

                         MARGARET

To the Next Door Neighbor

Dear Mrs. Swenson,

How are you? I am having a good time at camp. I miss hearing you yell at Mr. Swenson but I will be home soon.

Your neighbor,
LOUISE PEARSON

Dear Mom,

I wrote to Aunt Elsie, Uncle Max, Grandma Bea, Uncle Joel, Mrs. Gross, Cousin Larry, Mr. Valente and Grandma May like you told me too.

Now can I play some baseball?

Love and xxxx,
ALEXANDER

Dear Mom and Dad,

I wish Rover was up here at camp with me. He would like it, there are lots of trees here.

Love,
CYNTHIA

Dear Aunt Sophie,

I am having a good time. It is a lot of fun up here. Please pass this letter on to Aunt Ida, Uncle Morris, Cousin Mike, Aunt May, Uncle Henry, Cousin Joel, and Aunt Bea. Thank you.

Love,
EVELYN

Dear Mom and Dad,

   To save time, I am enclosing a postcard already written for every day that I am at camp.

                              Love,

                                        JACK

To Her Teacher

Dear Miss Brenner,

   I hope you have a nice summer and meet some man so you will be in a good mood when we come back to school.

                              Your pupil,

                                        JANET BUTTER

Dear Folks,

   This place is worse than a prison. It's like being back in school.

                              Your son,

                                        JEFFREY

Dear Mom and Dad,

   I'll bet if Wyatt Earp went to this camp he wouldn't like it either.

                              Love,

                                        JASON

A Letter Written on 8½ x 11 Paper

Dear Folks,

                              Love,

                                        BILL

Dear Dad,

We are going on a ten mile hike. Please send my bicycle.

PAUL

Dear Uncle Louie,

Mother wrote to me that you got married again. Is she as pretty as Aunt Emma? Where is Aunt Emma? How old is your new wife? I miss Aunt Emma.

Love,

JANET

Dear Folks,

This camp would be okay if they didn't have any girls here. All the girls can do is play volleyball. They shouldn't let girls go to camp. Why don't they stay home with their Mothers and do the dishes instead?

DON

Dear Mom,

I miss your yelling at me.

Love,

DIANE

Dear Folks,

Here are some pictures that I took of the camp. This is where we go to the bathroom and this is where they throw the garbage.

MICHAEL

To His Kid Brother

Dear Lewis,

Don't touch any of my toys till I get back.

Your brother,

MICKEY

Dear Mom,

I like camp better than anything except Captain Kangaroo.

Love,

MARVIN

Dear Grandma,

Please don't come up here anymore if you are going to cry when you see me.

Your grandson,

ROY

Dear Mom and Dad,

I am not going to go to college out of town if you have to write home as much.

Love,

JUDY

To His Best Friend Back Home
Dear Michael,

I am not going to write to you this summer until you answer the letter I sent you last summer.

TONY

Dear Dad,

This camp isn't like the pictures in the book that man showed us.

Your daughter,

RITA

Dear Mom,
   I miss you and Dad, and Grandma and Peter and Janie and my own TV set very much.

LOIS

Dear Folks,

I am trying to think of cute things to write so you can save my letters.

Love,

POLLY

To the Teacher

Dear Mr. Johnson,

I am having a wonderful summer. Are you having a good time? I am looking forward to going back to school. Please tell my Mother that I did write to you.

Your friend,

GRADE 7B (NEXT TERM)

To the Minister

Dear Reverend Jackson,

I hope you are having a pleasant summer. Camp is fun. We go to church every Sunday. The minister's name is Reverend Butter. Do you know him? He doesn't give as good a sermon as you do. You can hardly hear him. He doesn't talk loud like you do.

Love,

BETTY

Dear Aunt Fannie,

My Mother said I should write to you. How are you? That's good.

Love,

YOUR NEPHEW EDDIE

Dear Mom and Dad,
They should call this place Camp Sing Sing.
Love,

Kip

Two Letters from the Same Youngster

1st Day at Camp

Dear Folks,

The food is horrible. I don't like my bunkmates. I hate my counselor. Why did you send me up here?

Love, PETER

Last Day at Camp

Dear Folks,

I don't want to come home. Why are you making me come home?

Love, PETER

Dear Mom and Dad,

Please save all my letters so I won't have to write again next summer.

Love,

ELLEN

Dear Folks,

Please call me up on the telephone. I am too tired to write anymore.

Love,

HOWARD

Dear Mom and Dad,

It rained this week. Do you get a refund?

BETTY

Dear Folks,

We are having a good time. We made up a poem about the camp.

> Butter goes to bread
> Hammer goes to nail
> A comb goes to your head
> and
> This place is like a jail.

Love,

SHELDON

Dear Mom and Dad,

I am sending back the comic book you sent me. I read it. Please return it for another one that I didn't read.

GEORGE

First Day at Camp

Dear Mom,

I forgot to turn off the TV set in my room.

Love,

LOREN

Dear Sister,

I am having a good time. I miss you very much. I promise not to fight with you anymore when I come home. But you must promise not to be a pain in the neck.

Your big brother,

PHIL

Dear Folks,
It rained all last week. Don't pay them for that week.

Love,

EDITH

From the Same Youngster

1st Day
I am fine.

2nd Day
I am okay.

3rd Day
I am happy.

4th Day
I am swell.

5th Day
I don't know what else to write. I've told you everything already.

Love,

MARY

Dear Mom and Dad,
It's no fun up here. They don't have any television.

STUART

To His Teacher

Dear Mr. Saypol,
My Mother said I have to write to you so I am. Hello.

EVAN WRIGHT

Written to a Sick Aunt Obviously at the Request of Her Mother

Dear Aunt Gloria,

I hope you are feeling better so that soon you will be well enough to go down to the store to buy me something.

Love,

SALLY

Dear Dad,

Please send $6.35 for the wallet I made for you in Arts and Crafts.

Love,

PATRICIA

Dear Folks,

Please read this letter again tomorrow so I won't have to write again.

Your son,

MARTIN

Dear Grandma,

I miss you very much. Please send me a picture of you and Grandpa and also a box of candy.

Love,

ANN

Dear Aunt Jean,

I am not going to write to you any more. You have not sent me any candy all summer.

Love,

RITA

Dear Dad,

    I met a girl at camp and we are married. She is going to live in my room with me.

DEAN

71

Written on the Last Day of Camp by Different Youngsters

Dear Folks,

We had a real monkey as a pet in our bunk. We drew straws to see who would take the monkey home and I won. Aren't you proud of me?

Love,

MARTY

Dear Mom and Dad,

I am bringing a surprise home. Please have ten pounds of horsemeat ready.

Love,

JUDY

Dear Mother,

Don't be frightened if I look a little different when you see me.

Love,

ELAINE

Dear Parents,

You don't have to meet me at the bus station. My counselor said they are going to bring me home in a special car so I can lie down.

JASON

Dear Dad,

Tell Rover I am bringing home a friend for him.

Love,

LAURIE

Dear Mother,

I forgot how to make my bed already.

FRANCINE

Today, the modern camp offers everything but the Ballet Monte Carlo—and that's only because they are on tour during the summer.

From morning to night your offspring is kept plenty busy. There's no need for sleeping pills at camp. Even a banker who had given a million dollar loan to a man who just skipped the country could rest at camp. We ask you—what banker couldn't sleep after activities like the ones they write about on the following pages?

Dear Mom and Dad,

Yesterday we played hide-and-seek. I hid in the kitchen behind the stove. Don't tell anybody. I am still there.

Love,

JANET

Dear Mom and Dad,

Last night we had a real Indian campfire. I played the white hostage. They tied me up to a tree and built a big bonfire around me. I think I would rather be an Indian.

Love,

ARTHUR

Dear Folks,

Every day after lunch we have a nap period. I think it is a wonderful idea. I should do it at home after lunch instead of going right back to school. What do you think?

Love,

JEAN

Dear Mom and Dad,

They wouldn't let us shoot off any firecrackers for the Fourth of July because it is dangerous. So we had a big bonfire instead.

Love,

LAURIE

Dear Mom and Dad,
  Monday we played baseball.
  Tuesday we went rowing.
  Wednesday we went on a hike.
  Thursday we had a campfire.
  Friday we played tennis.
  Saturday we played basketball.
  Sunday we played volleyball.
  I am bored. There is nothing to do up here.

                    Your son,

                              FRED

Dear Mom,
  I just finished a wallet in Arts and Crafts. Please send me two dollars to put in the wallet so that it will look like a real wallet.

                    Love,

                              ALISON

Dear Mom and Dad,
  Yesterday we played catch-the-fly. I got eight flies. Here they are. Please save them for me. It is my new hobby.

                    Love,

                              EILEEN

Dear Folks,
  What kind of place is this? You have to sweep the floor, fix your laundry and make your own bed. I just came here to play baseball.

                    Love,

                              EUGENE

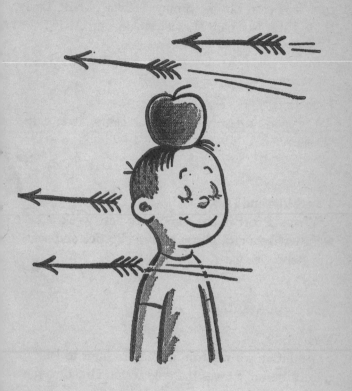

Dear Dad,

The boys in the bunk made up a new game. You try and hit an apple off some body's head with a bow and arrow. It's a lot of fun.

JACK

Dear Dad,

I am the best baseball player in the whole camp except for Peter, Bobby, Jimmy, Stewart, Mark, Larry, Billy, Paul, Norman, Howie, Jackie, and Alvin.

Love,

MARTIN

Dear Dad,

We made up a new game at camp. It is called "Destroy."

JIM

Dear Mom and Dad,

I have a part in the camp play next week. I have to dress like a girl. Please sent me lipstick and everything else girls wear.

Love,

STEWART

Dear Folks,

Yesterday we went on a treasure hunt to look for a lost treasure. It was the gold watch Grandma gave me for graduation.

Your son,

MICHAEL

Dear Folks,

I'm in a hurry. More tomorrow.

Your son,

DAVID

Dear Dad,

Yesterday I saw a real cow. It didn't look like Aunt Bertha.

Love,

SHIRLEY

Dear Mom and Dad,

Last night we slept out in the woods. I like it except when I had to go to the bathroom.

JERRY

Dear Mom and Dad,
  We learned a new camp cheer:

         Hipso Roso Teddy boom boom
                  boom
         Our camp is on the
                  Beam
         Hipso Rose Teddy ra ra
                  ra
         Our camp has the
                  team
         Hipso rase teddy cheer
                  cheer
         We want to come back next
                  year.
                       Love,

                            PATSY

Dear Uncle Max,
  I made you a pair of suspenders in Arts and Crafts
so your pants won't always look like they are falling
down all the time.

                  Your nephew,
                       DANNY

Hi:
  All the kids up here are trading baseball cards.
Please send me some more baseball cards. Don't send
any Mickey Mantle cards. You can't get anything for
them anymore.
                  Love,
                       GEORGE

Dear Folks,

We have to make our bed every day except for me because I sleep on the floor.

Love,

JOYCE

Dear Mom and Dad,

There is no television set at this camp. What kind of camp is this? How can I have any fun?

Love,

ROSLYN

Dear Aunt Dotty,

I like the nature hikes the best. Last week we caught all wild animals like a butterfly, a turtle, and two frogs but I wasn't afraid.

Your niece,

LESLIE

Dear Folks,

I am writing you an extra long letter today because I have time. We went to the lake yesterday and went swimming all day. Last night we played basketball.

Love,

ED

Dear Mom and Dad,

We went fishing yesterday and I caught a cold.

Love,

CHUCK

Dear Folks,

    I like it up here. They teach you how to do things. Last week I learned how to trap a skunk.

                         Love,

JAY

83

Dear Mom and Dad,

I got your letter and the answer to your question is I have been going every day.

Love,

CONNIE

Dear Dad,

They let us shoot rifles up here. Only we don't use real bullets any more since one of the boys was hit.

Your son,

GENE

Dear Dad,

Yesterday I went swimming. The watch you gave me is not waterproof like you said.

ROBERT

Dear Dad,

We went on a nature hike and I found where the poison ivy was.

Love,

JUDY

To His Big Brother in the Army

Dear Jim,

This camp is fun. How do you like the camp you are in? We played baseball yesterday. What did you do? Are you going back to your camp next summer?

Love,

PAUL

Dear Daddy,

Here is a picture of me swimming. You can't see me because I am underwater.

Love,

NANCY

Dear Mother,

We learned a new camp song. Here, I will sing it for you now. Do you like it?

Love,

JANE

86

Dear Folks,
   Guess which boy lost his new tennis racket?

SIMON

Dear Mom,
   When you come up to see me Sunday please bring:
                  a new tennis racket
                  three baseballs
                  a baseball bat
                  a snorkle
                  a football helmet
                  a basketball
                  track shoes
   Tomorrow I'll write you what else I need.

DEAN

Dear Folks,
   When it's very hot they let us go swimming without our bathing suits. Can we do that when we visit Uncle Herman at the beach?

Love,

JEFFREY

Dear Folks,
   We learned a new camp cheer. Want to hear it?
                  Hipzo rozo teddy boom bozo
                  I skidi, I skidi, I ski ski
                  Flubby dubb dubb dubb
                  ra ra ra ra ra.
                  Camp Hiawatha ha ha ha

DEBBY

87

Dear Dad,

Everybody in camp was given an Indian name. I am Chief Bald Eagle so guess what I did with my hair?

Love,

MARTY

8. Daddy

Dad holds a special position when it comes to camp. First of all, he paid for it (lest we forget). And secondly, it is within the tight community life of camp that children talk about their fathers more than ever.

"My Dad can climb the Empire State Building."

"That's nothing, my Dad built it."

Chest out, Dad. These letters are all about you.

Dear Mommy,
   My counselor sleeps all day like Daddy.
                              Love,

CHRIS

Daddy

Dear Dad,

When you come up to visit me again please don't bring your baseball glove. I don't want to play catch with you anymore. You are too old. Bring a book to read.

Love,

CONRAD

Dear Dad,

I told the girls in my bunk that you have more money than their fathers do. They don't believe me. Please send your bankbook so I can show them.

Love,

SUSAN

Dear Daddy,

Last week the other boys' fathers visited us. None of the other boys' fathers are bald. Next time you come up, please wear a hat.

Love,

JERRY

Dear Dad,

What size belt do you wear? I need to know because I am making you something in Arts and Crafts. It is a surprise.

Love,

JUDY

Dear Folks,

One of the kids in my bunk saw Daddy's picture and said he was fat so I hit him. I am sending back Daddy's picture.

Love,

YOUR SON PAUL

Dear Dad,

I am bringing a snake that I caught with me when I come home. Please don't tell Mother. I want to surprise her.

Love,

HENRY

Dear Dad,

Next Sunday the counselors are going to play the Fathers in a baseball game. Maybe you shouldn't come up.

BILLY

Dear Dad,

I hope you do good in the stock market next year so I can come back again next summer.

Love,

SUSAN

If a child learns one thing at camp, it's to share. It's not that they want to, necessarily—they are forced to.

Share and share alike is the motto of every bunk from Maine to California. Some kids learn to share gracefully. Others put up a fight.

Here are some ringside reports of the battle.

Dear Mom and Dad,

In our bunk the boys share everything. Today I am wearing Mickey's underwear.

MARK

Two Letters from the Same Youngster

Dear Mom and Dad,

I am the only one up here who ever gets candy from home. I am tired of sharing my candy with everyone else. Please send the candy inside my comic books so no one will know.

Love,

BETTY

SECOND LETTER TWO WEEKS LATER

Dear Mom and Dad,

Somebody took my comic books.

Love,

BETTY

Dear Folks,

One of the kids in my bunk borrowed my bathing suit. Please send me another bathing suit so I can have a suit to wear, too.

Love,

ELLEN

Dear Mother,

Betty is not my best friend at camp any more. She hasn't gotten a package from home in two weeks.

Love,

JUDY

Dear Mom,

I want to come home next week for my birthday so I can eat my birthday cake all by myself.

Love,

FRED

Dear Folks,

One of the boys in my bunk has a big sister like I do. He hates his sister, too.

Your son,

TIMMY

10. The Athlete

Not all children are good athletes. There are those youngsters who live for sports and those who could easily live without them.

It's not important how good an athlete the youngster is; it's more important the kind of athlete he is. It's better to be a good sport than good at sports or, at least, that's what my father always told me after the counselor broke the news to him that I was the worst softball player in the history of the game. Now, cheer up, your kid can't be that bad an athlete.

Dear Dad,

Next summer please send me to a camp where the pitchers aren't so good.

LIONEL

Dear Folks,

I won the award for the best softball player. Please send $50 for the trophy.

Your son,

MIKE

Three Letters from the Same Youngster

Dear Folks,

My team won in baseball. I want to be a baseball player when I grow up.

Love,

HOWIE

Dear Folks,

My team won in basketball. I want to be a basketball player when I grow up.

Love,

HOWIE

Dear Folks,

My team lost in baseball. I want to come home.

Love,

HOWIE

Dear Mom and Dad,

I can swim across the lake by myself. I did it last night after dinner when nobody was looking.

Love,

JACK

Dear Dad,

I still don't like camp. Are you sure Joe DiMaggio learned to play baseball at camp?

Love,

DAVID

Dear Dad,

I was elected Captain of the baseball team and now I need nine Hershey bars which I promised.

STEVE

Dear Mom and Dad,

This camp is awful. They make you take a bath every day.

RICHARD

Dear Dad,

I struck out with the bases loaded. I wish I was dead.

LARRY

Dear Dad,

I am going to learn to play golf. When my counselor plays golf he always lets me caddy for him.

ALEC

Dear Mom and Dad,
   I have joined the boxing club. This morning I had
my first fight. I don't think I will need braces for my
teeth any more.

Love,

JOHN

MONDAY

Today we played baseball and I got three hits. I like this camp.

TUESDAY

We played baseball and I hit a home run. I want to come back here again next year.

WEDNESDAY

I hit a double and a triple in the baseball game. This is the best camp I have ever been at.

THURSDAY

I made a double play in the baseball game. It's terrific up here.

FRIDAY

I struck out four times in the baseball game. I hate it up here. I want to come home.

Dear Mom and Dad,

Yesterday our camp played another camp in football. The other camp won. Next year I want to go to that camp.

Love,

GEORGE

To His "Big Brother"

Dear Peter,

They are teaching me how to box at camp. So you better run when I get home.

LIONEL

Dear Dad,

I love the horseback riding best of all. I am going riding again soon when I get out of the infirmary.

Love,

ELAINE

Dear Folks,

My favorite sport is swimming because when I go under water nobody can find me.

Love,

DAVID

Dear Dad,

I say my prayers every night but I still haven't hit a homerun.

Love,

ELIHU

Some of the strongest friendships many adults have grew out of acquaintances that began in camp.

Camp is a great place to get to know other children and to learn to like many different types of children.

It is not unusual for a youngster to return with forty new friends. Even the most withdrawn child is bound to come home with one or two playmates.

Despite what you have heard, the art of winning friends and influencing people really began on the third tennis court from the left one hot summer afternoon.

Dear Mom and Dad,

Next week we're going to have the election of the baseball team captain. I may win. Please send a new baseball to each of the boys in my bunk.

Love,

GEORGE

Hi!

When we come home next week all the girls in my bunk are going to meet over at our house. Please buy six cots so that we can all sleep together.

Love,

ANN

Dear Folks,

We have six kids in our bunk. Jimmy, who lives in Connecticut; Larry, who lives in Chicago; Peter, who lives in San Francisco; Stewart, who lives in Canada; Bobby, who lives in Atlanta and Howie who lives in Pennsylvania. When I come home I promised to visit all of them.

Love,

PAUL

Dear Mom,

When I get married, I want to spend my honeymoon at camp so I can be with my bunkmates.

Love,

GLORIA

Dear Folks,

Here is a picture of me with my best friend, Stanley. He looks funny because I just socked him.

Your son,

DONALD

Dear Mom and Dad,

I am in the infirmary because I got bitten by a snake. His name is Peter.

Love,

CHRIS

Dear Mom,

When I get home I want all the girls in my bunk to come sleep with me so I won't be lonely.

Love,

ELLEN

Dear Folks,

Here is a picture they took of me. The boy standing next to me with his arm around me is my bunkmate. He looks funny because he has poison ivy.

Love,

GARY

12. Clothes Make the Camper
—Anybody's Clothes!

There seem to be two unwritten laws among campers:

(a) Never return home with as much clothing as you left home with.

(b) If you *must* return home with some of the clothes you left with—

make sure you don't pack only your own clothes in your trunk.

Seasoned parents have long ago learned to anticipate receiving Jimmy Jackson's sneakers, Martin Lewis' toothbrush, Larry Gross' socks, and Peter Bumstead's handkerchief—all of which must dutifully be returned in the clothing exchange in which all parents participate two weeks after the camp season is over.

Dear Mom and Dad,

   We are having color war at camp. In color war the camp is divided into two teams. My team is the red team. The other team is the grey team. We paint all our shirts red. You'll love color war.

                                                        WALTER

You don't have to worry about my good pants not fitting next summer.

Love and xxx,

WARREN

Dear Mom,

Please send me some more handkerchiefs quick because I am all out of them and I have to blow my nose.

SAMUEL

Dear Mom,

It will be easier to pack my trunk when I come home because I won't have as many clothes to put in it.

Love,

MITCHELL

Dear Mom and Dad,

Our camp colors are red and gray so I had to throw away all my blue shorts.

Love,

ALICE

Dear Folks,

I am all out of socks and underwear. Please send me 24 more of each.

Love,

PETER

Dear Mom,

I lost my left sneaker but found another right sneaker. Please send me another left sneaker.

DICK

Dear Mother,

It is much easier packing my trunk coming home than it was when I left for camp. I hardly have anything to pack now.

Love,

KATHY

Dear Mom,

I am saving all my dirty laundry so I can bring it home with me for you.

Love,

MONTE

13. The Envelopes

Some of the most interesting things our youngsters write are on the envelopes of the letters they send from camp.

True, you can't tell a book by its cover. But ask any postman, and he will tell you all about your kid from the way he puts on the stamp, dots his "i" or spells his address. This is where child analysis really began.

Dear Postman:

I ran out of stamps. My Mother will pay you when she gets this letter. Say "hello" to her for me.

Dear Mr. Postman:

Please don't deliver between three and four o'clock because that is when my mother is at the laundromat.

House with the Crabgrass
Levittown, Long Island

Daddy's Office
Tallest Building in New York
New York City

Postman:

My phone number is Lehigh 5-3773. I don't know my address. Please look it up in the phone book.

Apartment 6R
New York City

Please deliver this letter
to the same house I sent the other letters.

Here is what my Mother looks
like.
Please give her this letter.

Please put in the mailbox with
all the bills.

Guess where this letter goes?

Envelope Addressed to His Kid Sister

Stupid
39 Oak Lane
Madison, Wisconsin

Postman:
   Please don't ruin this stamp because I want to use
it again.